LEE LAI

# STONE FRUIT

For Cesca,
my sister.

# CHAPTER ONE

THINGS WERE BEST WHEN NESSIE WAS ABOUT SIX.

WE WERE AT OUR BEST, FOR A WHILE, ANYWAY.

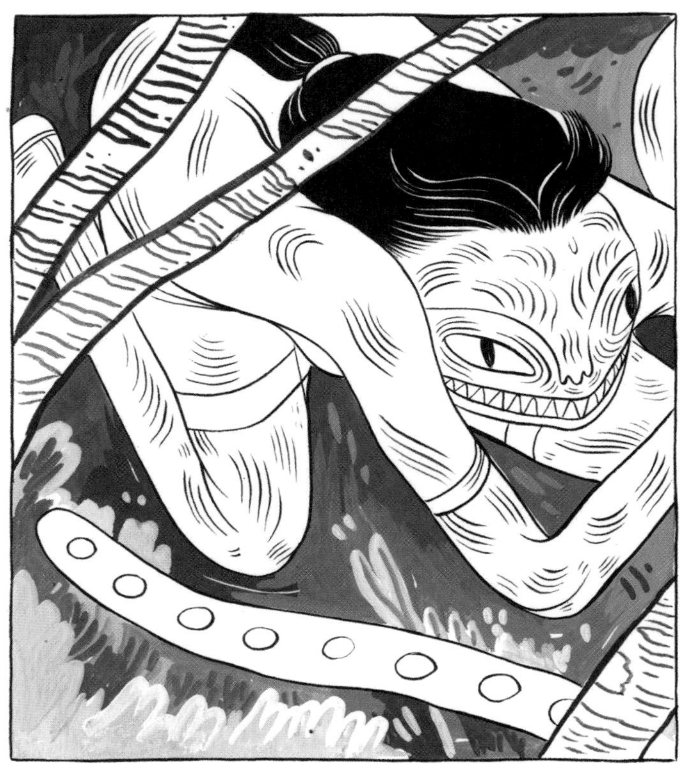

HE'S OVER THERE, I SAW HIM
GET HIM, BUB!

I THINK I GOT HIM!!!

GRASP

OOOOOFFF!

I FELL DOWN!
YOU FELL DOWN!

HI AMANDA, I WAS JUST — YES, YEAH OF COURSE SHE'S STILL WITH ME.
BRON TOO, YEAH. I — NO, WE WON'T BRING HER BACK COVERED IN — OK. TWO O'CLOCK? OK FINE.

OK, I GOT IT, AMANDA. I'M GOING TO GO NOW. I'LL SEE YOU SOON.
WE'RE AT THE MALL, SO WE'RE CLOSE.

WHAT'S THAT? I DON'T THINK IT MATTERS WHO—
OK, FINE, I'LL DRIVE. YES, I'LL DRIVE SAFE

I'LL TALK TO YOU SOON. BYE.

BEEP-

COME ON RAY!
OK COMING!!

HEY YOU TWO-

I DID ONE OF THOSE THINGS I TELL YOU NOT TO DO.
I LIED TO YOUR MUM, BUB, BECAUSE SHE WAS WORRIED AND I DIDN'T WANT HER TO BE.

SO, JUST SO SHE DOESN'T GET UPSET, WE SPENT TODAY IN THE LANGLEY MALL, YOU KNOW WHAT I MEAN?
YEP OK!

LET'S GO BACK TO OURS QUICK AND CLEAN YOU UP.
BRUSH

DON'T WORRY EVERYONE, WE'LL CATCH THAT LITTLE BASTARD SOON.
BRON.
SORRY.

THERE SHE IS!

IN YA SEAT, SWEET PEA, SO I CAN BUCKLE YOU IN

OH IF I WAS A FROG
OH IF I WAS A FROG
I'D WIFE ME A SNAKE

CUZ A FROG WITHOUT A SNAKE - CAN'T GET NO BREAK

OH IF I WAS A FROG I'D WIFE ME A SNAKE CUZ A FROG WITHOUT A SNAKE CAN'T GET NO BREAK—
NOO I DON'T WANNA BEEE, THIS FROG NO MORE

YOU'RE LATE.

—NEARLY THREE, NOW.

I DON'T KNOW AMANDA, YOU WANT ME TO BE ON TIME BUT DRIVE SLOW—
PICK

IS SHE IN THE CAR?
YOU MEAN BRON? SHE'S IN THE CAR, YEAH.

HM. SHE MIGHT'VE COME UP AND SAID HELLO, ANYWAY.
OH PLEASE, LIKE YOU EVEN CARE ABOUT SAYING HELLO.

... YOU'RE ALWAYS RUSHING TO ASSUME THE WORST OF ME, YOU KNOW THAT?
MAYBE IF YOU OPERATED ON A LEVEL OF BASELINE RESPECT, I WOULDN'T BE SO QUICK TO—
OH, YOU'RE ONE TO TALK ABOUT BASELINE RESPECT.

JUST BECAUSE YOU WANT TO BE HELPING OUT, DOESN'T MEAN YOU CAN FEEL ENTITLED TO TELL ME—
HELPING OUT?!
YOU REALLY WANT TO HAVE A CONVERSATION ABOUT ENTITLEMENT, AMANDA? REALLY?

YOU NEED TO STOP—
...OH IF I WAS A FROG, I'D WIFE ME A SNAKE...

I LOVE AUNTIE BRON.
I WISH SHE COULD SLEEP OVER IN MY ROOM SOMETIMES.

... I DON'T THINK THAT WOULD BE APPROPRIATE, BABY.
LET'S SAY BYE TO AUNTIE RACHEL AND GET YOU CLEANED UP, YOU'LL SEE HER AGAIN THIS SATURDAY.

SHE **IS** CLEAN, AMANDA
I **AM** CLEAN, MUMMA!

... I'LL TEXT YOU ABOUT WHEN TO COME ON SATURDAY.

SLAM
SIGH

HOW'D IT GO?

SLAM

SHE'S--JUST...SEARCHING-
FOR ANYTHING TO CON-FIRM THAT I'M A-I'M-

IT'S LIKE SHE'S TESTING ME.

...

OHH IF I WAS A'MANDA-
I'D JUMP IN A LAKE
SOOO THIS DREAMY OLD BEAST
CAN CATCH A BREAK-

NO I DON'T WANNA BEEE-
THAT MUMMA NO MOORE

... TAKE ME HOME AND ROLL AROUND IN BED WITH ME, BABE?

VRRRRRRR

SORRY FOR YELLING BACK THERE, BABY.

IT'S OK, YOU TWO ALWAYS SHOUT AT EACH OTHER.

... EAT YOUR RICE, NESS.
SO, DID YOU HAVE FUN WITH AUNTIE RACHEL TODAY?
PUSH
AND AUNTIE BRON, MUMMA.
AND AUNTIE BRONWYN.

WE HAD **SO MUCH FUN**, WE WENT TO THE **LANGLEY MALL**
... YEAH, RACHEL MENTIONED THAT. SO WHAT DID YOU GET UP TO OVER THERE?

OH, STUFF.

OH... WAS IT BORING?
NO!! I LOVE SPENDING TIME WITH AUNTIE RAY AND AUNTIE BRON!!
SO WHAT DID YOU LOVE DOING?
JUST STUFF, MUMMA.

... WHAT WAS THAT FUN SONG YOU WERE SINGING BEFORE?
OH, JUST A SONG THAT AUNTIE BRON MADE UP.
OH YEAH? HOW'D IT GO?
NO, YOU GOTTA MAKE IT UP ON THE SPOT.

OK, WANT TO MAKE UP A SONG TOGETHER WHILE WE EAT?
I'M NO GOOD AT IT, AUNTIE BRON AL-WAYS MAKES THEM.
OH.

KITCHEN.

BEDROOM

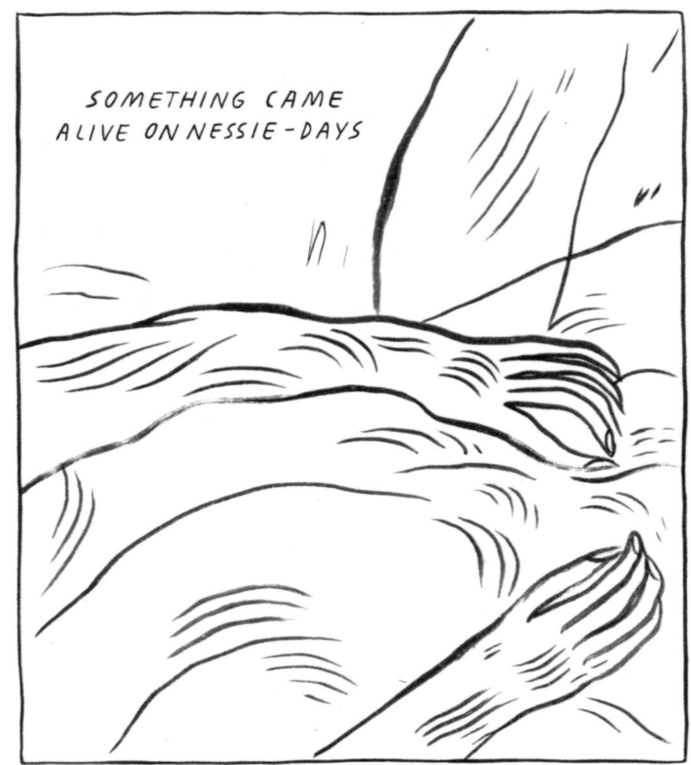
SOMETHING CAME
ALIVE ON NESSIE-DAYS

BRON WAS HAPPY.

(TRAFFIC SOUNDS)

WHEN WE STARTED OUT, BRON WOULD TEASE ME ABOUT BEING A TOUGH NUT TO CRACK.
BUT SHE CRACKED ME, WITH HER CHARM AND HER HUMOR AND HER PATIENCE.

SHE WAS SO SOFT AND SO FUCKING SWEET THAT IT WAS HARD TO BE ANYTHING ELSE, WHEN I WAS WITH HER.

BUT AS TIME PASSED, AS WE GOT CLOSER, I REALIZED THERE WAS SOMETHING HARDER, IN HER, DEEPER IN THERE.

AND I HAD NO IDEA WHAT TO DO WITH IT.
HEY.
DID YOU SLEEP OK?

MM, SLEPT FINE.
... ARE YOU OK?
I'M FINE.

DO YOU STILL WANT TO HANG OUT AFTER WORK?

SURE.

WE DON'T HAVE TO DO MUCH. WE CAN JUST WATCH A MOVIE IF YOU'RE FEELING WEIRD.
OR, WE CAN WORK ON THE GARDEN, LIKE WE SAID.

SURE, WHICHEVER, I DON'T CARE.
YOU DON'T CARE?

SORRY, I DIDN'T MEAN— ... IT'S EARLY. CAN WE JUST MAKE COFFEE?

I CAN'T DO IT LIKE THIS. EVERY MORNING.

WHAT DO YOU MEAN?
I CAN'T DO THIS THING EVERY MORNING WHERE I HAVE TO GAUGE WHAT I CAN EXPECT FROM YOU, AND THEN DIG IT OUT OF YOU.

I DON'T KNOW WHAT YOU EXPECT.
THIS ISN'T NEW SHIT, BRON. WE'VE BEEN THROUGH THIS SO MANY TIMES.

I'M NOT EXPECTING YOU TO BE, SUDDENLY, YOU KNOW, HAPPY ALL THE TIME.
BUT IT'S LIKE, EVERY MORNING I FEEL LIKE THERE'S... JUST... ALL THE EGGSHELLS.

I TOLD YOU IT WOULD BE LIKE THIS. YOU CAN'T MAKE IT GO AWAY OVERNIGHT.
YOU SAID YOU WERE DOWN.

I AM, BUT I STILL NEED TO ASK FOR THINGS, BABE.
WHAT ARE YOU ASKING FOR?
I... UM-

I CAN'T JUST FIX ALL MY SHIT, RAY. IT'S A MESS, MY SHIT'S A MESS.
I CAN'T HAVE YOU TRYING TO FIX ME.
I'M NOT TRYING TO FIX YOU.

IT REALLY FEELS LIKE IT SOMETIMES.
JESUS, BRON, I'M JUST WANTING YOU TO TAKE CARE OF ME TOO.

I'M TRYING.
I KNOW YOU ARE

I DUNNO IF IT'S GOOD ENOUGH FOR YOU.
BRON...
I GOTTA GO TO WORK. I'M LATE. SORRY.

BABE.

FOLLOWING THESE
KINDS OF MORNINGS

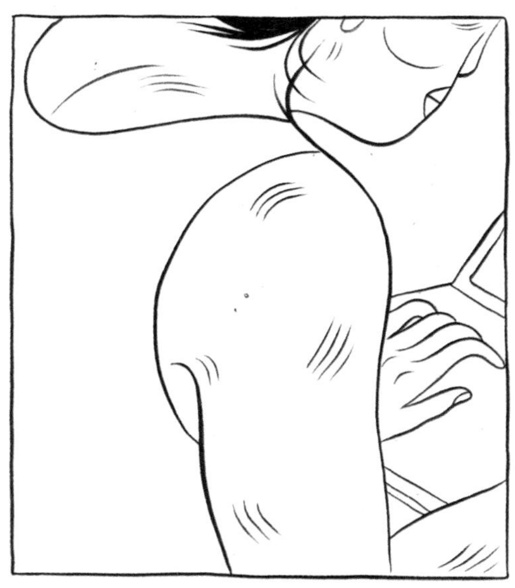

CRUN
CH

RESISTING THE URGE TO TEXT HER
THROUGHOUT THE DAY

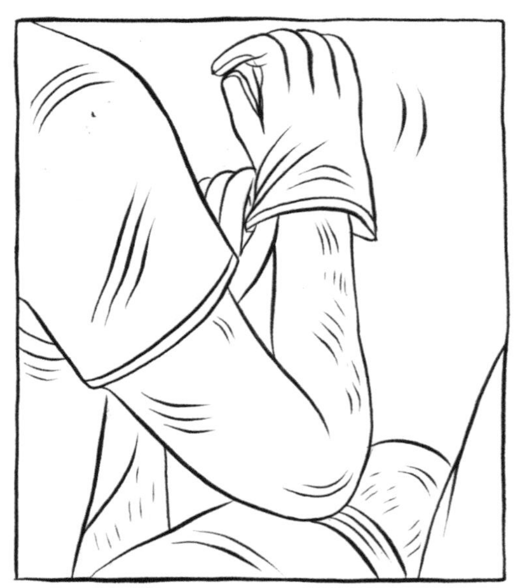

BUT I MANAGED.

...CAN I TOUCH YOU?
YEAH.

I'M SORRY. I DON'T KNOW HOW TO NOT BE LIKE THIS RIGHT NOW.

I KNOW.
I CAN'T STAND IT, RAY. SOMETHING HAS TO CHANGE.
I KNOW.

BRON... CAN YOU TELL ME THAT "SOMETHING" DOESN'T MEAN ME?
IT DOESN'T.

CAN YOU... COULD YOU SAY THAT AGAIN FACING ME?

IT DOESN'T MEAN YOU.

# CHAPTER TWO

♩ OH IF I WAS A RAT ♩
OH IF I WAS A RAT

I'D LIVE IN THE TREES
'CUZ A SCARY-ASS RAT
CAN DO WHAT SHE PLEASE

AUNTIE BRON! I CAN'T SING THEM WITH MUMMA LATER IF THEY HAVE SWEAR WORDS IN THEM.

WHAT? WHAT'S THE RUDE WORD THERE?
"ASS"
"ASS" IS A SWEAR?

HUH. IF "ASS" IS A SWEAR, YOUR MUM IS GONNA HAVE A RUDE AWAKENING WHEN YOU TURN FIFTEEN, DARLING.

I WONDER IF AMANDA WOULD THINK THAT ROARING IS A SWEAR
. . .

OOA
OOAARK
OOOOOA

OOORA
OOOOO

OA
OVER HERE

WAIT FOR THE ECHO, BUB!

OHH IT VIBRATES IN MY INSIDES.

THANKYOU, GHOSTS, FOR SINGING WITH US.

STRETCH
THIS HILL IS THE PERFECT HILL!

THANK YOU GRASS, FOR BEING SOFT FOR OUR BODIES.
FLOP

THANK YOU BEES FOR BEING ALL AROUND US BUT NOT STINGING US.
THANK YOU LUNCH FOR BEING IN MY BELLY.

THANK YOU HILL!
FOR BEING SLOPEY!

THANK YOU SKIN, FOR HOLDING EVERYTHING TOGETHER.

THANK YOU RAY
FOR BEING SO PATIENT. DESPITE FUCKIN' EVERYTHING.

AUNTIE BRON, AUNTIE RAY!!
NESSIE??
WHERE—

SHHH — HERE!!

OOOHYES

THERE HE IS.

...STEADY, BUB.

WHAT THE HELL??
SCAM-
PER
GOD, SORRY, WAIT—
RRRINGG!

IT'S AMANDA, I GOTTA TAKE IT.
OOAAA AHW!!

HELLO - AMANDA? WAIT, I CAN'T HEAR YOU -

LLO? OK, IT'S GOOD NOW - WHAT'S UP

OH IF I WAS A BADGER...
I'D EAT LOTS OF BISCUITS —

...BECAUSE A BADGER NEEDS — TO EAT LOTS OF BISCUITS...

AUNTIE BRON? WHAT'S WRONG?

HEY DARLING, THAT WAS YOUR MUM. SHE'S ANXIOUS TO HAVE YOU HOME EARLY SO WE'RE GONNA HEAD HOME NOW, OK?
WHAT??

NOOO IT'S STILL EARLYYY!
SEE? SHE DOESN'T WANT TO GO.
IT'S NOT UP TO US, BRON.

WHY IS IT NOT UP TO US, THOUGH? DOES SHE CON-SIDER FOR EVEN A MINUTE THAT THIS REALLY MESSES WITH US??
BABE.

CAN WE NOT DO THIS NOW? PLEASE?
I HAVE TO TAKE US HOME. I JUST WANT IT TO BE EASY TONIGHT.

SHE DOESN'T GET TO TREAT EVERYONE LIKE THEY'RE INFERIOR. SHE DOESN'T GET TO TREAT YOUR TIME LIKE IT DOESN'T MATTER, LIKE THIS DOESN'T MATTER.
BRON! CAN YOU PLEASE CALM DOWN?

I'M NOT GOING TO JUST ADJUST TO HER WHILE SHE GOES ON BEING A MANIPULATIVE FUCKING TYRANT!
BRON, WHAT THE HELL, STOP!!

AUNTIE BRON?

CAN WE GO HOME?

JUST ACKNOWLEDGE IT'S CONTROLLING!!

"TRYING TO CONTROL YOU," CHRIST. YOU MAKE ME OUT TO BE SOME KIND OF MONSTER, LIKE MY INTENTIONS AREN'T ALWAYS WITH NESSIE'S BEST-
OH, LIKE YOU ALWAYS KNOW WHAT NESSIE'S BEST INTERESTS ARE.

OH, AND YOU DO? YOU THINK YOU KNOW ABOUT PARENTING FROM SOME PART-TIME INSIGHT, BUT YOU DON'T EVEN KNOW THE HALF OF IT.

I WANTED HER TO COME HOME EARLY SO SHE COULD WIND DOWN A BIT. YOU DROP HER HOME AND SHE'S HYPER, RAY, AFTER SHE'S SPENT THE WHOLE DAY WITH BRON—
SO THIS IS ABOUT BRON.
THAT'S NOT WHAT I SAID. DON'T PUT WORDS IN MY MOUTH.

AND DON'T YOU PISS ME AROUND, AMANDA! YOU ALWAYS FIND A WAY TO UNDERMINE ME AND BRON'S TIME WITH NESSIE.
IT WASN'T THE AGREEMENT. IT WAS SUPPOSED TO BE YOU LOOKING AFTER HER, NOT YOU AND HER.

SO WHAT IS IT THEN? IT'S FINE IF I'M ALONE, BUT YOU DON'T WANT TO HAVE NESSIE GETTING ALL CORRUPTED BY SEEING NASTY, FREAKY QUEER LOVE?

YOU'RE JEALOUS OF HER. YOU'RE THREATENED BY HER BEING DIFFERENT FROM YOU AND YOU'RE THREATENED THAT NESSIE ADORES THE SHIT OUT OF HER —

SHE IS DIFFERENT! YOU'VE TOLD ME WHAT SHE CAN BE LIKE — SHE'S SICK IN THE HEAD! SO YES, SHE'S DIFFERENT.
AND I THINK THAT'S BAD FOR NESSIE.

I THINK SHE'S BAD FOR **YOU**.

SHIT, BRON—

...

MAYBE IT'S TIME TO GO, RAY. IT'S GETTING LATE.

BRON... WHEN AMANDA GETS UPSET, SHE BACKS HERSELF INTO A CORNER -
- THEN LASHES OUT AND SAYS THE MOST HURTFUL THING SHE CAN THINK OF. SHE'S BEEN DOING THAT SINCE WE WERE BOTH KIDS.

THE BEST THING TO DO IS IGNORE HER.

BABE?

IT'S OK. I CAN IGNORE IT.

DID YOU HAVE A FUN TIME TODAY?

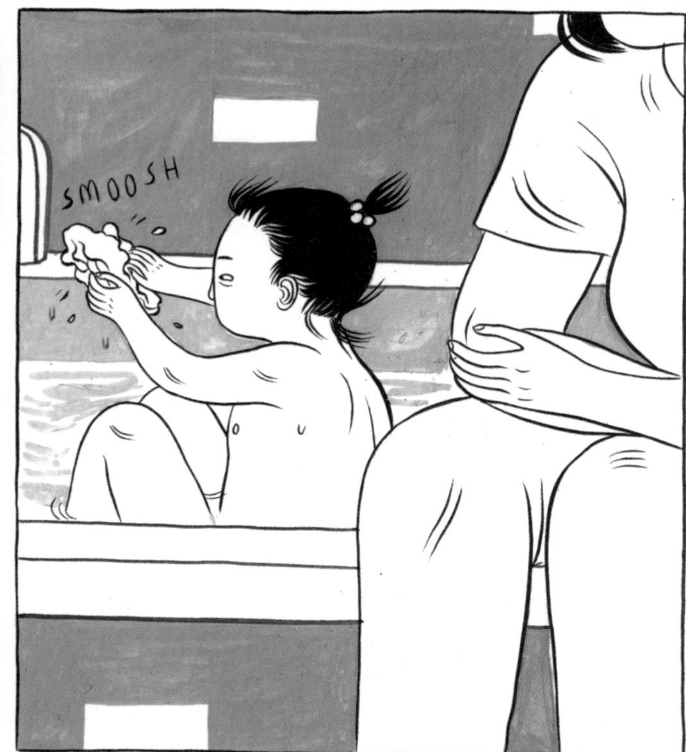
SMOOSH

I'M SORRY I CUT YOUR PLAY-DATE SHORT TODAY, LOVE. ONE OF MY CLIENTS CAN-CELLED AND I WANTED TO HAVE YOU HOME SO WE COULD HAVE BATH-TIME...

...AND MAYBE WE CAN WATCH A MOVIE, BECAUSE I'M GOING TO BE WORKING LATE TOMORROW, SO...

... DO YOU... DON'T YOU WANT TO SPEND TIME WITH ME TOO, BABY?

DON'T BE SAD, MUMMA.
I WANNA WATCH A MOVIE WITH YOU.

OH, SORRY, I DIDN'T —
UHH— —

I DIDN'T KNOW YOU WERE OUT HERE. I'LL JUST — I'LL BE IN THE BEDROOM.

WHO WERE YOU TALKING TO BEFORE?
JUST A FRIEND.

OH, WAS IT ANDER?
NO.

...ARE YOU TALKING TO YOUR FAMILY AGAIN?

WHY?
I DUNNO, I WAS JUST CURIOUS, I GUESS...
SORRY, I FEEL LIKE I'M PRY-ING. I'M GONNA STOP ASKING.

... BRON? CAN WE TALK ABOUT THE ONE MILLION THINGS TODAY THAT WERE AWFUL AND WEIRD?

I'M TIRED, BABE. I CAN'T HANDLE IT TONIGHT, I'M SORRY. DO YOU WANT TO CUDDLE?

YEAH.
I WAS THINKING. MAYBE NEXT TUESDAY WITH NESSIE WE CAN GO BACK TO THE SAME SPOT. THERE'S ACTUALLY HEAPS OF PARKLAND THERE WE HAVEN'T SEEN YET.

BRON... I THINK THAT – I DONT KNOW. I FEEL LIKE THINGS WITH AMANDA ARE AT THE BREAKING POINT RIGHT NOW...
...MAYBE I SHOULD JUST TAKE NESSIE BY MYSELF ON TUESDAY. JUST 'TIL THINGS... YOU KNOW –

I CAN'T BELIEVE YOU.
I'M NOT SIDING WITH AMANDA. SHE HASN'T GOTTEN TO ME. IT'S JUST – TODAY WAS REALLY HARD, BABE.

BRON, PLEASE.
I'M SLEEPING ON THE COUCH.

WE LASTED ABOUT FOUR MONTHS FROM THAT POINT.

IMPRESSIVE, ACTUALLY, ALL THINGS CONSIDERED.

WE WERE BOTH HANG-ING OUT FOR THOSE TUESDAYS AND SATUR-DAYS WITH NESS.

THEY WERE LIKE LITTLE ISLANDS OF SOLACE —

IN A TIME THAT I THINK WE BOTH CAME TO REMEMBER AS AN OCEAN OF SHIT.

HI, DAD?
YEAH, IT'S ME. YOU GOT TIME TO TALK?

AND THEN, YOU KNOW –

THE WINTER STARTS ROLLING IN, AND IT'S A MONDAY AND IT'S RAINING...

AND BRON JUST GETS UP AND SAYS –

I HAVE TO GO, RAY.

WHAT DO YOU MEAN? WHERE?
WHY ARE YOU LOOKING AT ME LIKE THAT?

IT'S BEEN MONTHS, RAY. I HAVE TO GO AND DEAL WITH —
THIS

YOU'RE DEALING WITH IT. HERE.
I'M NOT, RAY. YOU'RE DEALING WITH ME —

I HAVEN'T BEEN DEALING AT ALL.

YOU SAID YOU WANTED ME TO BE BETTER —
WAIT, BRON, I DIDN'T SAY IT LIKE THAT.
— AND I'M TRYING, RAY. THIS IS ME TRYING.

BRON, WHERE ARE YOU GOING?

WELL... SO, I HAVE BEEN TALK-ING WITH MY FAMILY. WITH DAD.
I'M GOING TO STAY WITH THEM. FOR A LITTLE.

WITH YOUR DAD??
MR. BREAD-AND-WINE BAXTER? BABE, WHAT THE HELL.
RAY, PLEASE.

WHAT HAVE THEY BEEN TELL-ING YOU? DID THEY TELL YOU TO MOVE BACK IN?
YOU KNOW, WHEN YOU ASK QUESTIONS LIKE THAT, YOU SOUND A HELL OF A LOT LIKE THEM.

BUT I... OK. UM...

I'M STAYING WITH THEM FOR A WHILE, TO TALK, AND THINK—

—AND, JUST... GET MY HEAD RIGHT.

BABE, THEY DON'T EVEN USE YOUR NAME RIGHT.
TUCK

I DON'T GET IT. YOU SAID YOU DIDN'T WANT TO GO TO THERAPY.

YOU SAID YOU WERE GOING TO FIGURE IT OUT WITH YOUR PEOPLE. AND... FIGURE IT OUT WITH ME.
AND MY FAMILY DON'T COUNT AS MY PEOPLE?
YOU HAVEN'T TALKED FOR FOUR YEARS. THEY HAVEN'T BEEN THERE FOR YOU.

...YOU CAN'T SAVE ME, RAY.

NEITHER CAN JESUS.
I KNOW THAT.
DO YOU, THOUGH?

EVERYTHING'S JUST BEEN... FUCKING AWFUL. FOR AGES. WE BOTH KNOW IT. I DON'T KNOW WHAT ELSE TO SAY.

YOU FUCKIN' PROMISED — THAT NEEDING SOMETHING TO CHANGE WOULDN'T MEAN ME.
IT DOESN'T MEAN YOU

THEN WHAT IS THIS? DO YOU WANT ME TO WAIT FOR YOU? DO YOU WANT ME TO VISIT? ARE YOU COMING BACK?

I ... UM, I DON'T KNOW. MY DAD, HE WOULDN'T ... UH —

I JUST HAVE TO GO FOR A BIT.
I DON'T KNOW WHAT I WANT. I JUST HAVE TO GO.

BRON WAIT —

CAN WE JUST GO TO – I DUNNO, A DINER OR SOMETHING, AND TALK?
...I'VE CALLED A CAB, RAY.

I DON'T KNOW WHAT TO SAY YET. I'M SORRY. I JUST HAVE TO GO FIX ...THIS.
ZIP

OK...

OK.

YOU DON'T HAVE TO —
I SAID I WAS DOWN, SO I GUESS THIS IS BEING DOWN, RIGHT?

I'LL WAIT, IF THIS IS WHAT YOU HAVE TO DO.

WILL YOU CALL ME? WILL YOU SEND ME EMAILS, CAN YOU TELL ME HOW YOU'RE GOING?
I DON'T... I JUST NEED TO CLEAR MY HEAD.
WHAT DOES THAT MEAN? SHOULD I LEAVE YOU ALONE? WHAT DO YOU NEED?

I DON'T KNOW.

BRON—
I'M SORRY IF I'VE BEEN AN ASSHOLE.
ME TOO.

BRON, WE'RE FINE, RIGHT? YOU JUST NEED SOME TIME?

I LOVE YOU. I'M SORRY.

OK.
OK.

OK...

WHAT THE FUCK

# CHAPTER THREE

HEY, YOU'VE REACHED BRON —

YOU KNOW WHAT THE DEAL IS. MAKE IT CUTE IF YOU CAN —

— I'LL GET BACK TO YOU SOON. BEEP'S COMING IN A SEC —

BEEP

– YOU'VE REACHED BRON –

... KNOW WHAT THE DEAL IS.
MAKE IT CUTE...

... BEEP'S COMING IN A SEC...

... HEY, YOU'VE REACHED –

BABY, JUST CALL ME, OK? OR TEXT. I JUST WANNA KNOW HOW YOU ARE.

I COULD COME VISIT. OR I CAN JUST GIVE YOU SPACE.

FLOP

JUST LET ME KNOW.

KNOCK
KNOCK

KNOCK
KNOCK

KNOCK
KNOCK
KNO

KNOCK
KNOCK
KNOCK

WHAT'S GOING ON RAY, I'VE BEEN CALLING YOU FOR —
HI AUNTIE RAY!

- GOD, YOU LOOK LIKE HELL. WHAT HAPPENED TO YOU?
JESUS CHRIST, IS IT TUESDAY?
YES, RAY. TODAY. TUESDAY. ELEVEN O'CLOCK. YOU HAVEN'T SEEN ANY OF MY CALLS HAVE YOU.

HAVE YOU BEEN DRINKING?!
NO, GOD, OF COURSE NOT. I JUST... I HAVEN'T BEEN SLEEPING SO WELL.

... I CAN'T MAKE OTHER ARRANGEMENTS, I'VE GOT A CLIENT COMING IN HALF AN HOUR.
IT'S FINE, I'VE GOT IT.

WE'RE GONNA HAVE FUN, RIGHT? WE GOT THIS.
WE GOT THIS!!

OKAY, CALL ME. OR I'LL CALL YOU AFTER THIS CLIENT.
I KNOW YOU WILL.

SIGH
OK BE GOOD!!
YESSSSS!!

ROOORROOO o
YAROOOOOO

LOUISA SHOWED US A SONG ABOUT ELENA-BEAR AT DAYCARE, AUNTIE RAY! I WANNA SHOW YOU!

SHE WAS YELLOW LIKE HONEY AND BIG LIKE THIS!

... WHERE'S AUNTIE BRON?

SHE'S NOT HERE TODAY, BUB. IT'S JUST YOU AND ME TO-DAY, IS THAT OK?
WHERE IS SHE? IS SHE SICK?
SHE'S NOT FEELING HER BEST, YEAH. SHE'S, UH, GONE TO SEE WHAT SHE CAN DO ABOUT THAT.

... OK. ARE WE GOING OUT FOR TODAY?
NO, I - UHM, I THINK WE SHOULD HAVE A HOME-DAY TODAY.

... DO YOU WANNA HEAR ABOUT THE HONEY-BEAR?
I REALLY DO, BABY.
LET'S GO IN THE GARDEN? WE CAN BE ELENA-BEAR IN THE GARDEN.

OK, ARE YOU READY?
WE HAVE TO MAKE OUR-SELVES BIG LIKE ELENA-BEAR TO DO THE SONG.

RIGHT... OK...
AUNTIE RAY!

YOU HAFTA PUT YOUR ARMS OUT LIKE THIS.
RIGHT, YES. HERE WE GO.
OK, SO THE VERSE GOES:
ELENA-BEAR IS A YELLOW-ER BEAR-

CUZ SHE LIKES TO EAT THAT HO-NEY
AUNTIE RAAAY!

I—I HAVE TO...
I'M SORRY BABY, I GOTTA CHECK SOMETHING.

"O NEW MESSAGES"

ALRIGHT. FUCKIN' COME ON.

OK DARLING, I'M GOOD TO - UH -
AUNTIE RAY? WHAT'S WRONG?

IT'S FINE, EVERYTHING'S FINE -
WHERE'S AUNTIE BRON? WHERE IS SHE?
SHE'S, JUST, NOT HERE

WHEN IS SHE COMING BACK??
I DON'T KNOW
BUT WHERE IS SHE??

I DON'T KNOW NESSIE, SHE'S JUST NOT HERE!

...

WWAAAAAAAA!!!

SLAM!

CLATTER

HI MUM
OH, YOU'RE STILL— I THOUGHT YOU'D BE DONE. SORRY.

WAIT IN YOUR ROOM BUB, YOU CAN WATCH T.V. AND MUM'S GONNA FIND YOU IN A BIT, OK?
I'M SO SORRY ABOUT THIS.

OK, I'M DONE NOW. WHAT THE HELL IS GOING ON.
SHE'S GONE, AMANDA
BRON'S GONE AND I CAN'T FUCKING COPE

WHAT? WHAT DO YOU MEAN? DID SHE WALK OUT?
NO, NOT LIKE THAT. SHE'S, LIKE... HAVING A BREAKDOWN... OR SOMETHING.
SHE WENT TO STAY WITH HER FAMILY AND THEY'RE ... JUST... WASPY CHRISTIAN MANIACS —

SHE'S GOT SO MUCH SHAME TO DEAL WITH, AND SHE WENT THERE TO CLEAR HER HEAD AND THEY'RE GONNA MAKE HER SO MUCH WORSE
AND I DON'T KNOW WHEN SHE'S COMING BACK. I DUNNO IF SHE'S COMING BACK.

OH.

...
PAT

CAN YOU TAKE NESSIE FOR A FEW TUESDAYS AND SATURDAYS? I FEEL LIKE I'M BREAKING APART, AND I DON'T WANNA UPSET HER—
... DON'T BE STUPID, RACHEL.

WHAT?
THIS ISN'T ABOUT UPSETTING NESS. WHAT YOU'RE ASKING FOR IS TO SHIRK YOUR RESPONSIBILITY SO—YOU CAN FALL APART.

N-NO, THAT'S NOT WHAT... I'M SAYING I JUST NEED A SEC—
YOU'RE **SAYING** THAT YOU WANT TO DISAPPEAR INTO SOME **HOLE** BECAUSE YOUR DAY GOT A BIT HARDER—
SO YOU CAN JUST POP UP WHEN YOU'RE READY, AND BE FUN AND LIGHT AUNTIE RAY AGAIN.

YOU THINK I GET TO BE FUN AND LIGHT FOR NESSIE EVERY DAY?

WHEN DAVE WALKED OUT, I CRIED EVERY DAY FOR THREE WEEKS. IT FELT LIKE THE WORLD WAS ENDING.
AND NESSIE SAW MOST OF THAT, BUT I DON'T THINK I **RUINED** HER OR ANYTHING.

I STILL GOT HER UP, AND FED, AND DRESSED. EVERY DAMN DAY.

AND THEN YOU STEPPED IN, EVEN THOUGH WE HADN'T TALKED SINCE DAD DIED, AND YOU SAID YOU WERE **DOWN**.
DO YOU KNOW WHAT DOWN MEANS?

IT MEANS CUTTING UP TOAST SOLDIERS WHEN YOU HAVEN'T SLEPT PROPER IN A WEEK. SINGING TIMMY-THE-TORTOISE OR WHATEVER THE HELL WHEN YOU FEEL LIKE YOU'RE CHOKING.

...
THIS DOESN'T GET TO BE LIKE, "LET'S SWOOP IN AND TAKE BABY OFF TIRED OLD MUM'S HANDS, AND IT'S ALL **FUN** AND **MAGICAL** ALL THE TIME."

YOU SAID YOU WANTED TO BE FAMILY AGAIN.

THIS IS IT.

SO I'LL SEE YOU NEXT SATURDAY.

YOU DON'T HAVE TO BE FUN,
MAGICAL AUNTIE RAY.

YOU JUST NEED TO SHOW UP.

SAN
HOT
MEALS

AND YOUR LEG?
OPEN
HOURS

STILL HURTS, BUT A LOT BETTER AFTER THE OPERATION. WE'LL HAVE TO MOVE EVENTUALLY, THE STAIRS WILL GET TO ME AT SOME POINT.
MATTHEW THINKS WE SHOULD BE DOWNSIZING ANYWAY.
RIGHT. THAT MAKES SENSE.

WE, UH, PACKED UP YOUR ROOM. A COUPLE OF YEARS AGO.
OPEN
24 HOURS
WE GAVE A LOT OF THE STUFF TO THE ST. VINCENT'S IN TOWN. YOU DIDN'T SEEM TO WANT YOUR OLD CLOTHES...

WE DIDN'T THINK YOU'D MIND.
IT'S FINE, I DON'T MIND.

BUT AFTER YOU CALLED, MATTHEW AND I SWAPPED THE COUCHES IN THE BASEMENT AND THE LIVING ROOM, SO YOU CAN HAVE THE SOFA-BED.
GRACIE HAS YOUR OLD ROOM NOW. SHE SAID YOU COULD SHARE HER BED WITH HER IF YOU'D FIT. WE ASSUMED YOU'D PREFER SOME PRIVACY, OF COURSE.

SHE'S EXCITED YOU'RE COMING HOME, SHE'S MISSED HER BIG—
... WELL. SHE'S MISSED YOU.
OPEN
24 HOURS

HOW'S MUM?

OH, SHE'S DOING WELL. I KNOW SHE MISSES THE KIDS — NOT THE OTHER TEACHERS SO MUCH. SHE KEEPS HER-SELF BUSY WITH THE VOLUNTEERING.
SHE'S WORKING WITH SOME OTHER WOMEN AT ST. MARK'S, THEY'RE PUT-TING TOGETHER AN INTER-FAITH PROGRAM AT THE RESOURCE CENTER — WITH ALL THE MULTI-CULTURAL ACTIVITY IN THE NEIGHBORHOOD, YOU KNOW. SHE'S KEEPING BUSY.

HAVE YOU TOLD HER? THAT I'M COMING.
OF COURSE.
AND... WHAT DOES SHE THINK?

WELL, YOU KNOW THERE IS ALWAYS A PLACE FOR YOU IN THE FAMILY HOME.
ALL DONE HERE?

TWO BILLS?
JUST ONE, PLEASE.
THANKS, DAD.

HEY, DAD?

I'M SORRY. FOR LAST TIME.
I NEEDED TO LEAVE, BUT I DIDN'T NEED TO SAY ALL THOSE THINGS.

WE DON'T HAVE TO TALK ABOUT THOSE THINGS.

THERE'S SO MUCH, THAT I HAVEN'T TOLD YOU ABOUT.

YOU DON'T HAVE TO TELL ME EVERYTHING, YOU KNOW.
I KNOW. I MEAN — IT'S JUST STUFF I THINK YOU'D ACTUALLY... JUST, THINGS I'D LIKE TO TELL YOU.

...THERE'S THIS KID IN MY LIFE. SHE'S NOT MINE, IT'S NOT LIKE THAT, BUT... YEAH. WE SPEND A LOT OF TIME TOGETHER
AND SHE'S WONDERFUL

WHO ARE HER PARENTS?
UHM, THIS WOMAN CALLED AMANDA IS HER MUM
AND HER FATHER?
HE'S NOT AROUND.
HMM.

... AND AMANDA'S SISTER IS RAY, SO RAY'S THIS KID'S AUNTIE.
SO I'VE KIND OF BEEN HER AUNTIE, TOO.

RAY. IS THAT...?
UH, YEAH. SHE WAS THE ONE THAT CAME AND PICKED ME UP... LAST TIME.
THAT ANGRY CHINESE GIRL.

I MEAN, YOU COULD EASILY SAY THAT YOU AND MUM WERE THOSE ANGRY MIDDLE-AGED ANGLOS IN THAT ENCOUNTER.

...

...BUT ANYWAY. THIS KID, HER NAME IS NESSIE. SHE'S SIX, AND A BIT SMALL FOR HER AGE.
BUT SHE'S LOUD AND VIBRANT AND VERY IMAGINATIVE.

SHE'S A GOOD LEADER WITH GAMES. WHEN SHE'S AT DAYCARE, SHE GETS THE OTHER KIDS TO ENTER THESE, LIKE, SCENES —OR WORLDS—WITH HER.
IT'S LIKE SHE KNOWS HOW TO GET EVERYONE FEELING AS EXCITED AND FREE AS SHE IS.

SHE'S SO... WEIRD. AND EMOTIONAL. AND JUST, VERY FULL OF LOVE. AND SPIRIT.

...SHE SOUNDS LIKE HOW YOU WERE,
WHEN YOU WERE THAT AGE.

I GUESS SO, YEAH.

AUNTIE RAAAAAYY!

THE EPISODE IS PLAYING AGAIN.
HM?

OH, RIGHT. SORRY—UH—
DO YOU WANT TO PUT ON ANOTHER ONE?
I WANNA DO SOMETHING ELSE.

I WANT TO FIND THE SILVER DOG. I WANT TO GO OUT AND LOOK FOR HIM.
I DON'T KNOW HOW TO FIND HIM WITH-OUT BRON LEADING THAT CHASE.

SHE... SHE COULD SPOT HIM BEST.
I KNOW.
... ARE YOU SICK? YOU LOOK LIKE YOU'RE SICK.
NO, I JUST HAVEN'T HAD MUCH SLEEP, SO I'M FEELING ... SLUMPY. SORRY, SWEET-PEA, I KNOW I'M NOT MUCH FUN RIGHT NOW.

OH. IT'S OK.
YOU'VE BEEN SLUMPY FOR A WHILE. IS IT BECAUSE YOU'RE SAD?
I... WELL, YES.

YEAH. I MISS HER, TOO.
ALL IS WHALES
WHERE ARE YOU—?

WHAT HAVE YOU GOT THERE?
...THEY'RE A BIT BAD OKAY?
'CAUSE YOU'RE REALLY GOOD AT DRAWING AND I'M REALLY BAD.

WHAT DO YOU MEAN?
I DREW SOME STUFF WITH YOU AND ME AND AUNTIE BRON AND THE BIG BROWN RIVER WHERE WE WERE LAST TIME, BUT I MESSED IT UP.
THAT'S VERY SWEET, BUB. CAN I SEE?

...BUT IT'S ALL SCRIBBLED OUT.
I TOLD YOU I MESSED IT UP!

BUT NOW YOU CAN'T SEE WHAT YOU DID.
ALL IS WHALES
IT HELPS IF YOU CAN STILL SEE THE THINGS THAT YOU'VE MESSED UP.
YOU ALWAYS KNOW WHAT YOU'RE DOING.

HAHA
WHAT?
NEVER MIND
ALL IS WHALES
HERE, DO YOU WANNA TRY AGAIN TOGETHER?

OK. I'LL DO THE COLORING BITS.
SO—
— WE WERE ON THE BANKS OF THE BIG BROWN RIVER —

TREES, TREES TREES TREES. MORE, AUNTIE RAY.
AND YOU CAN DRAW YOU HERE. AND AUNTIE BRON HERE.

... AUNTIE RAY? HERE.
ALL IS WHALES
RIGHT... SORRY—YES, OK —

OK, OK, SO—
AUNTIE BRON SAID WE SHOULD LOOK AROUND THE RIVER THIS TIME—

SHE SAID MAYBE THE FISH WOULD KNOW WHERE THE SILVER DOG IS.
REMEMBER?

"THE SNAPPERS IN THERE COULD TELL YOU THINGS THAT'D MAKE YOUR TOE-NAILS CURL"— YES, I REMEMBER.
Km/h

SO WE NEED A BOAT —
BIGGER THAN THAT, AUNTIE RAY!
GOT IT.

AND WE'RE ALL IN THE BOAT, AND
THE WATER'S ALL FROTHY AND WAVY —
BUT IT'S A RIVER, BUB,
AND IT'S STORMY NOW, WATCH OUT AUNTIE RAY!

CLOUDS! WIND!

A BIG STORM IS COMING
WITH RAIN AND LIGHTNING

WE'RE HOME

WE ALL HAFTA HOLD ON!!

AUNTIE BRON'S FALLEN OVER THE SIDE!!
WHAT??
ALL IS WHALES

IT'S OK, SHE CAN SWIM.
DRAW HER SWIMMING.

HERE.
ALL IS WHALES

SHE'S JUST GONE TO TALK TO THE FISHES AND CRABS AT THE BOTTOM.

YOUR HAIR IS SO LONG NOW.
YOU'RE SO DAMN TALL NOW.

HI MUM...
DO YOU... WANNA HUG?

AAALRIGHT, LET'S GET YOU SET UP.

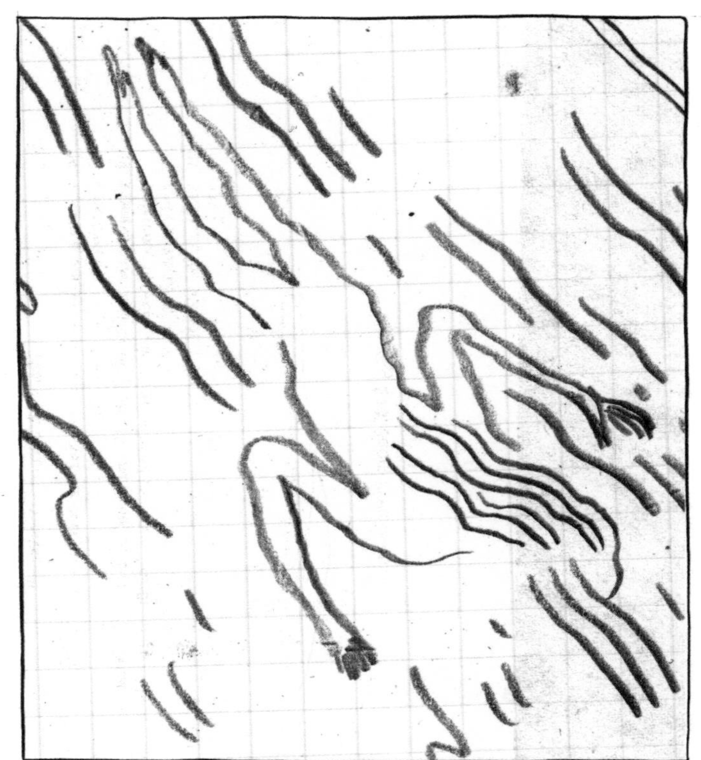

THE WATER'S GETTING MORE CALMER, DON'T WORRY—
WE JUST HAFTA WAIT UP HERE.

RRRINNG
SHIT, WHAT'S THE TIME? HOLD ON —

HEY YOU SWORE!
AMANDA, HEY.
FIFTEEN? OKAY.

YOUR MUM'S ON HER WAY TO COME PICK YOU UP, MY LOVE.
TIME TO PACK UP.

THANKS FOR TODAY.
YOU KNOW, YOU'RE STILL FUN, EVEN WHEN YOU'RE SLUMPY.
OKAY. THANKS.

YOU LOOK THIN.
ARE YOU EATING?
I'LL HAVE SOMETHING WHEN I GO BACK UPSTAIRS.

ALSO, AUNTIE RAY—?
YEAH?
THE FISHES TOLD AUNTIE BRON WHAT'S UP: SHE SAID THAT THEY SAID THAT THE SILVER DOG WAS HANGING OUT WITH THEM FOR A BIT. BUT NOW HE'S HIDING SOMEWHERE ELSE.

MAYBE WE CAN TRY THE CAVES NEXT TIME!

CHAPTER FOUR

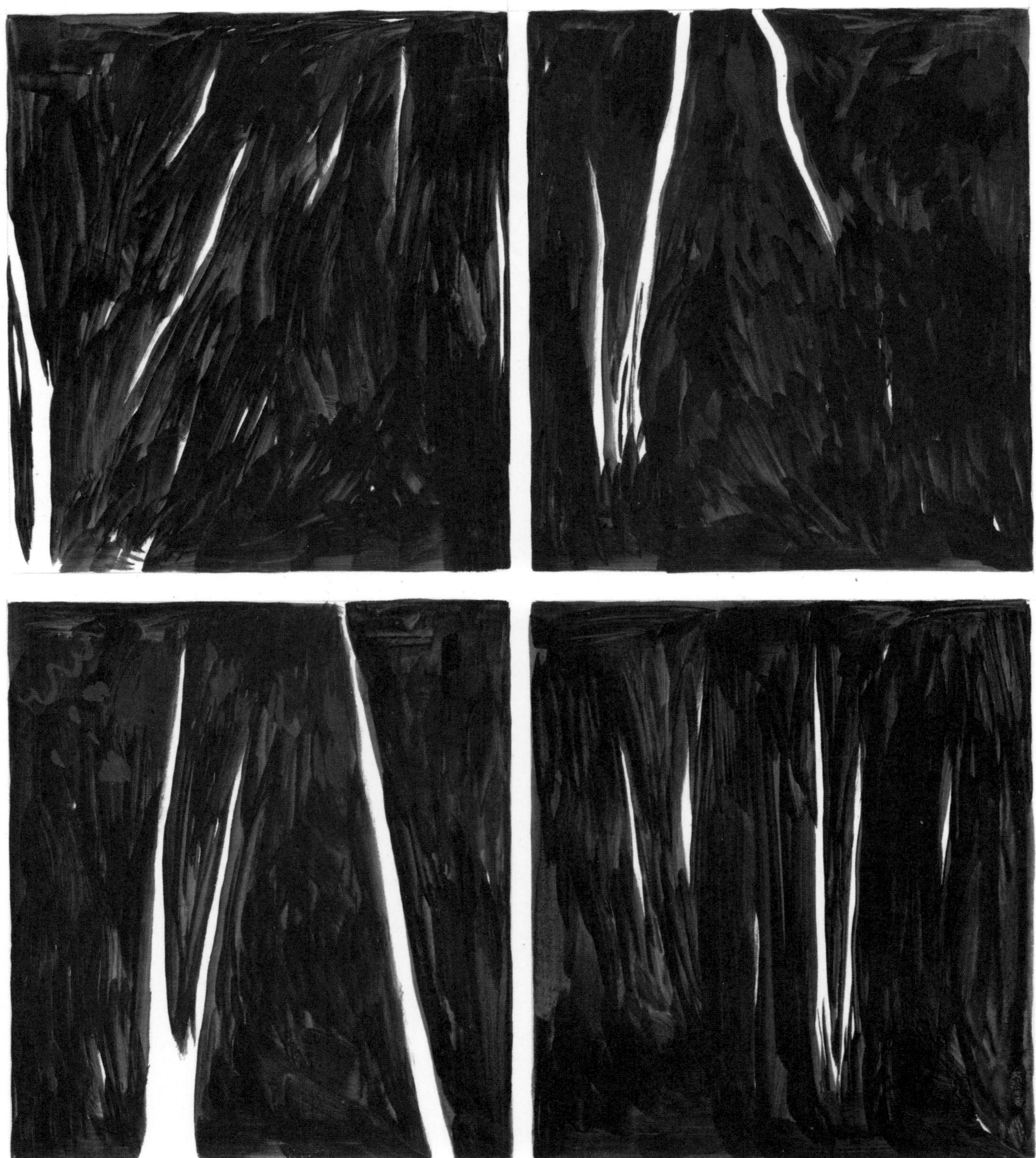

BRON!!
STUMBLE

WHAT ARE YOU DOING HERE?

BRON, BABY—
YOU GOTTA MOVE.

I CAN'T MOVE.
YOU CAN, YOU JUST NEED TO—

I DON'T WANT TO.

GODDAMMIT—
JUST TAKE MY HAND, BABE, YOU HAVE TO MOVE!!

I DON'T WANT YOU.

BRON, PLEASE—

I DON'T WANT YOU

I DON'T WANT YOU!
I DON'T WANT YOU!!

I DON'T WA—
K-KEUUGGH!

NO!!

GASP–

GULP

CHRIST.

YOU KNOW, YOU CAN STOP FREAKING OUT THAT YOU'RE BURDENING EVERYONE WITH YOUR FREAKY PRESENCE.

THEY'RE HAPPY YOU'RE HOME.
REALLY.

I KNOW THEY'D LIKE, NEVER EVER SHOW THEIR EMOTIONS UNLESS YOU RAN NAKED THROUGH THEIR LIVING ROOM SCREAMING "GOD IS A LIE," OR SOMETHING.
BUT THERE'S LITTLE THINGS. TRUST ME.

HMM.

HEY, I'VE BEEN AROUND HERE LONG ENOUGH TO MAKE A SOCIAL STUDY OUT OF THOSE TWO. I'M AN EXPERT.
I KNOW. I KNOW I LEFT YOU HERE ON YOUR OWN WITH THEM.

IT'S OKAY. MAYBE IT'S THE SECOND CHILD THING, THEY'RE WAY MORE CHILL WITH ME THAN THEY EVER WERE WITH YOU.
YOU WANT ANY OF THIS GRANOLA THING?
NO, I'M GOOD.

SO YOU'RE NOT UPSET AT ME?
NO.

YOU SEEM UPSET AT ME.

I THINK I JUST... I DON'T KNOW, YOU'RE JUST SO MUCH COOLER AND WEIRDER THAN ME —
PICK
— I THINK I JUST WANTED TO SEE SOME OF THAT COOL WEIRD LIFE YOU WERE LIVING, Y'KNOW, FINDING YOURSELF OUT IN THE REAL WORLD.

LIKE WHAT ARE YOU EVEN DOING BACK HERE, YOU KNOW?

HA ... I GUESS, FINDING MYSELF.
WELL THAT'S WEIRD.
YEP.

ALSO, LET'S BE CLEAR — YOU'RE DEFINITELY BOTH COOL AND WEIRD.

AND THERE'S NOTHING STOPPING YOU FROM TAKING OFF WHEN YOU'RE READY.
I'M NOT LEGAL-ANY-THING YET.
AND I DUNNO, I FEEL LIKE I GOTTA STICK AROUND FOR MUM AND DAD.

PLUS - AND THIS SOUNDS SO DUMB, I KNOW -
BUT LIKE, I DON'T KNOW WHAT IT MEANS TO JUST TURN AWAY FROM EVERYONE AND... EVERYTHING. IT'S NOT LIKE IT'S MY WHOLE LIFE, BUT...

...
SHRUG

AND THEN EVERY TIME I MEET KIDS IN OTHER YOUTH GROUPS, THEY'RE JUST TOTAL SQUARES.
I DON'T EVEN KNOW WHERE I'D FIND PEOPLE WHO ARE JUST... COOL. WHO WON'T EXPECT ME TO LIKE, DISAVOW EVERYTHING I KNOW.

...WHAT?
...I'VE NEVER APPRECIATED BEFORE THAT WE'RE ACTUALLY KIND OF ALIKE.

YEAH THAT'S 'CUZ THE LAST TIME WE WERE HANGING OUT I WAS TWELVE AND ALL I WANTED TO TALK ABOUT WAS PONIES OR WHATEVER. I HAVE A WHOLE PERSONALITY NOW.

YOU HAVE SO MUCH CATCHING UP TO DO.
IT'S TRUE.

...SO YOU'RE GOING TO STICK AROUND THEN?
I'D LIKE TO.

WHAT ABOUT THAT GIRL? YOU WERE TOGETHER, RIGHT?
RAY. YEAH, WE WERE TOGETHER. I THINK I'VE RUINED IT, THOUGH.

WHY?
WE'VE BEEN LIVING TOGETHER. AND I'VE BEEN SUPER DEPRESSED AND LOST AND JUST... I'VE BEEN DRAGGING HER DOWN.

AND THEN I GOT SICK OF FEELING GUILTY AND HOPELESS, SO I THOUGHT THE BEST THING WAS JUST TO... REMOVE MYSELF.
AND I MADE A MESS OF LEAVING.

SHE DIDN'T WANT ME TO, BUT SHE ALSO WASN'T HAPPY WITH THE WAY THINGS WERE. AND SHE WAS JUST SO HELL-BENT ON BEING THE REASON, IN SOME WAY, THAT I GOT BETTER.
I COULDN'T HACK IT.

BUT YOU STILL LOVE HER, HEY.
SO MUCH.

AND YOU'VE BEEN TOGETHER WHAT, LIKE FIVE YEARS?
YEAH.
THAT'S FOREVER!
I GUESS SO...

BUT SHE WAS SO DETERMINED TO BUILD THIS LIFE THAT LOOKED THIS ONE PARTICULAR WAY, AND I DIDN'T KNOW WHERE TO PUT ALL THE PARTS OF ME THAT I LEFT BEHIND WHEN I MET HER.

I DON'T THINK SHE WANTED TO KNOW ABOUT THOSE PARTS, EITHER.
I'VE FELT SO TORN.

... WELL, THIS IS ALL WAAAY BEYOND MY MATURITY LEVEL —
HA, FUCK, SORRY, I DIDN'T MEAN TO SAY ALL THAT.

BUT IT'S DEFINITELY BETTER THAT YOU'RE TALKING ABOUT IT WITH ME THAN WITH MUM AND DAD. THEY'D JUST LOOK AT YOU LIKE YOU'RE A TERRIFYING ALIEN.
THEY ALREADY LOOK AT ME LIKE I'M A TERRIFYING ALIEN.

GIVE THEM TIME. LIKE OBVIOUSLY YOU'VE CHANGED A LOT.
BUT THERE'S ALL THESE BITS OF YOU THAT ARE EXACTLY THE SAME.

THEY'LL FIGURE IT OUT.

WHEN I MET BRON, WE BONDED ABOUT HOW ALONE WE BOTH WERE.

MY RELATIONSHIP WITH MUM WAS WHATEVER, DAD WAS DEAD, AND AMANDA WAS SHACKED UP WITH NESSIE AND THAT DOUCHEBAG DAVE.

MOVING BRON OUT OF HER FAMILY HOME WAS LIKE THE RUSH OF A JAILBREAK.

WE SET UP THE APARTMENT FOR THE TWO OF US, AND ALL WE TALKED ABOUT WAS CHOOSING OUR OWN FAMILY AND LIVING EXACTLY HOW WE WANTED TO LIVE.

AND THEN ALL THAT SHIT GOES DOWN WITH AMANDA AND DAVE, AND THEN NESSIE'S IN OUR LIFE ALL OF THE TIME, AND BRON...

I DON'T KNOW HOW TO EXPLAIN IT —

SHE'D BECOME LIKE, MORE HAPPY THAN I'D EVER SEEN HER. AND MORE SAD, AT THE SAME TIME.

AND ALL THE STRUCTURES WE'D BUILT TOGETHER SUDDENLY FELT UNBEARABLY FRAGILE.

RAY?
WHAT ARE YOU DOING HERE?

WELL, HI YOURSELF.

WHERE DID YOU PARK? I ONLY GOT HOME TEN MINUTES AGO, THERE WASN'T EVEN SPACE FOR MINE—
I WALKED HERE.
WHAT? THAT'S A TWO HOUR WALK!
WOW, YOU REALLY MUST BE IN BREAKUP MODE.

THAT'S NOT WHAT — IT'S NOT LIKE THAT—
WELL, I'M SORRY TO DISA-PPOINT AT THE END OF YOUR GREAT PILGRIMAGE—
—BUT NESSIE'S ON A PLAY-DATE WITH ONE OF THE KIDS FROM DAY CARE THIS AFTERNOON. SHE WON'T BE HOME FOR A FEW MORE HOURS.

ACTUALLY, I CAME TO SEE IF YOU'D LIKE TO HANG OUT.

HANG OUT? WITH ME?
YEAH.
YOU WANT TO HANG OUT WITH ME.

GOD, YOU MAKE IT SOUND LIKE SOMETHING PERVERSE.
...
COME ON, WE DON'T HAVE TO PAINT TOENAILS AND SPILL SECRETS OR WHAT-EVER. CAN WE JUST, SIT IN THE KITCHEN AND HAVE A CUP OF TEA OR SOMETHING? I PROMISE I WON'T CRY THIS TIME, EITHER.

LOOK, I PICKED UP A BAG OF THOSE TAPIOCA CHIPS THAT YOU LIKE.

...ALRIGHT, FINE, COME IN.

HI MUM...

IS IT OK IF JOIN YOU?
YES, THAT'S FINE.

THEY'RE ALL READY TO GO, HEY?
I SHOULD HAVE PULLED THEM OUT AND COMPOSTED WEEKS AGO, THE WINTER'S REALLY ON ITS WAY NOW.

I CAN HELP, WE CAN MAKE A TIME SOON—
IT'S ALL RIGHT.
I'D BE HAPPY TO, THOUGH—

NO, I CAN MANAGE.
I KNOW WHAT I'M DOING, REALLY.

I DON'T NEED HELP, I CAN HANDLE IT ON MY OWN. THANK YOU.

OK... SHOULD I GO RIGHT NOW?
NO, IT'S ALL RIGHT—
YOU CAN HELP ME PRUNE THE PERENNIALS NOW.

... I'VE BEEN WORKING FOR A LAND-SCAPING COMPANY FOR THE PAST TWO YEARS.
OH, WELL, THAT'S GOOD. YOU'VE ALWAYS BEEN DRAWN TO GREEN SPACES.

YEAH, THAT'S TRUE. I'VE WANTED TO GET INTO BUSH AND FORESTY BITS MORE THOUGH, 'CUZ WORKING IN PARKS DOESN'T QUITE CUT IT, REALLY.
IT'S FEELING DOABLE, TOO — I HAVE ACCESS TO A CAR NOW, AND THERE'S THIS KID IN MY LIFE—

YES, YOUR DAD TOLD ME ABOUT HER.
OH. OK.
...WELL, YEAH. SHE LIKES WILDER GREEN SPACES, TOO.

WHAT DO YOU DO IN THE WINTER?
WHAT DO YOU MEAN?
FOR WORK. WHEN THE WINTER SETS IN.

OH... WELL, IT'S SEASONAL, SO I GUESS THERE'S USUALLY A FEW MONTHS WHEN I'M OUT OF WORK.
THOSE MONTHS ARE HARD. THINGS GET A BIT... WEIRD. WHEN I'M OUT OF WORK.

ACTUALLY, MUM, I'VE WANTED TO ASK YOU —
I WANTED TO TALK ABOUT THOSE PERIODS. WHEN I WAS SAD.

WHAT DO YOU MEAN?

I MEAN... I USED TO BE WORSE. THAN I AM NOW.
I WANTED TO ASK WHAT THAT WAS LIKE FOR YOU.

YOU WOULD REMEMBER THOSE TIMES BETTER THAN ME, I'D THINK.
YOU TALKED TO FATHER WILLIAM SEVERAL TIMES A WEEK, AND YOUR DAD AND I INVESTED IN THE PSYCHIATRIST THAT HE RECOMMENDED FOR YOU.

I DON'T THINK THERE IS MUCH MORE TO SAY.

BUT... I NEED TO KNOW WHAT IT ACTUALLY FELT LIKE, FOR YOU TWO.
I NEED TO UNDERSTAND—
THERE'S NOTHING TO UNDERSTAND.
WHAT DO YOU MEAN? DIDN'T IT BOTHER YOU THAT I WAS— WEREN'T YOU WORRIED?

OF COURSE WE WERE WORRIED.
OF COURSE IT BOTHERED US.
BUT CLEARLY YOU HAVE DONE SOME WORK ON YOURSELF, AND LIVING ON YOUR OWN AND DOING WELL IT SEEMS—

SO I DON'T KNOW WHAT MORE THERE IS TO SAY.
I WASN'T LIVING ON MY OWN.

THERE WERE THINGS THAT FATHER WILLIAM SAID...
MADE ME THINK THAT YOU MIGHT HAVE GONE THROUGH THIS TOO.

THROUGH WHAT.
I WAS IN THIS SUPPORT GROUP FOR A WHILE —
AND THEY TOLD ME IT'D BE HELPFUL TO LOOK INTO MY FAMILY FOR A HISTORY OF MENTAL ILLNESS.

WE DON'T HAVE A HISTORY OF MENTAL ILLNESS IN OUR FAMILY.

WHAT, AND I'M JUST THE ONLY FUCKED-UP ONE IN A LONG LINE OF GOD'S JOYFUL CHILDREN?!
DON'T BE DRAMATIC. YOU'VE JUST BEEN MISGUIDED.
THAT DOESN'T HELP ME, MUM.

NOBODY TALKS ABOUT THEIR FUCKING FEELINGS HERE.
I DON'T KNOW HOW YOU DON'T ALL JUST EXPLODE.

I DON'T KNOW WHAT YOU CAME HOME LOOK-ING FOR.

I'M GOING TO START ON DINNER.

WHAT ARE YOU DOING??
I'LL BE THIRTY SECONDS! JEEZ.

HERE. LOOK WHAT I FOUND.

NO... WHERE WAS THIS?
GREAT AUNTIE MAY'S 80TH BANQUET, I THINK. SHE'S THE ONLY ONE WHO EVER ORDERED SCALLOPS – YOU CAN SEE THEM IN THE BACKGROUND.

OH MY GOD – LOOK AT YOUR FUCKING BRACES!
I KNOW.
LOOK AT MY HAIR.
THAT WAS YOUR "EVERYONE IN THE WORLD MUST KNOW THAT I'M A HUMONGOUS DYKE" PHASE.

PRETTY MUCH.
WOW, DAVE. HE LOOKS LIKE SUCH A BABY HERE, NO FACIAL HAIR.

I KNOW. I DON'T THINK WE'D EVEN HAD SEX AT THIS POINT.
YEAH, YOU'D JUST DRY-HUMP IN THE BACK OF HIS MUM'S TOYOTA AFTER HIS BASKETBALL GAMES.

WHY DIDN'T YOU SHOW ME THIS BEFORE?
ARE YOU KIDDING??

THIS IS THE FIRST TIME IT'S BEEN JUST THE TWO OF US IN... I DON'T KNOW. YEARS. WITHOUT NESSIE, OR – WELL–
OR BRON.
WELL, YES.

AND... I GUESS I HAVEN'T KNOWN WHAT TO SAY TO YOU IN YEARS.

OTHER THAN CRITICISMS AND UNSOLICITED OPINIONS, YOU MEAN?
YOU DON'T EXACTLY INVITE OPENNESS.
NEITHER DO YOU!

... WELL, DIDN'T WE TURN OUT EXACTLY LIKE MUM, THEN.

I'M GOING FOR A SMOKE.
FINE. DO IT OUT THE BACK, THE NEIGHBORS ARE JUDGEY ABOUT THAT KIND OF THING.
NO, I MEAN—DO YOU WANNA SMOKE WITH ME.

OH—RIGHT...
UH, SURE.

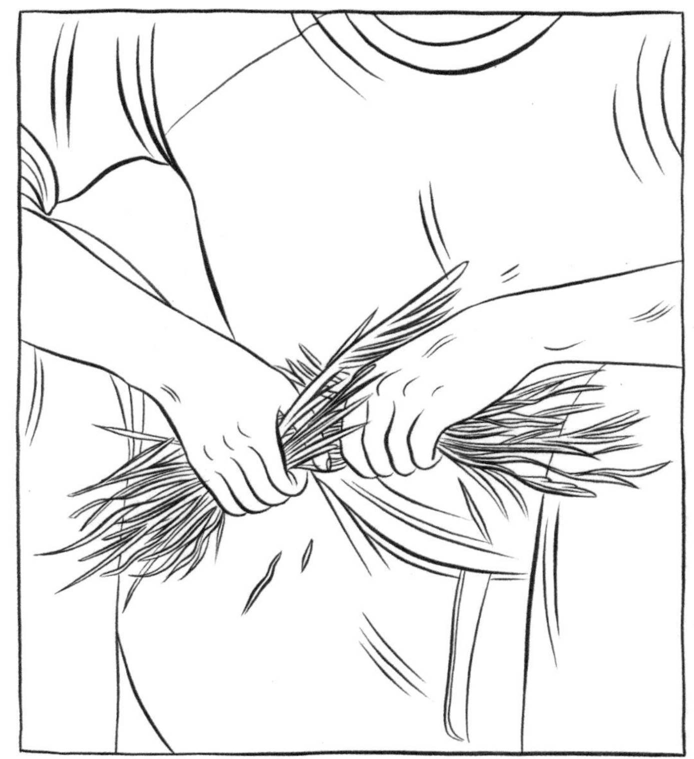

HEY.

...

...JUST GIVE HER TIME.

CHAPTER FIVE

THE FIRST TIME BRON AND I FOUGHT, IT WAS OVER SOMETHING INCREDIBLY TRIVIAL.

WE'D SPENT A FULL FIVE DAYS TOGETHER, AND
WE WERE GIDDY WITH THE NEW FEELINGS
OF FAMILIARITY AND INTIMACY.

SOMEHOW WE'D ESTABLISHED
THAT I'D NEVER IN MY LIFE
EATEN A NECTARINE, SO
BRON MADE IT HER MISSION
TO FEED ME ONE AS
SOON AS POSSIBLE.
VERT

WE WENT TO THE STORE
AND THEN SAT ON THE CURB, AND
SHE STARTED DOING THAT
THING THAT SHE DOES.

HERE, LOOK AT THE COLOR FIRST. LOOK AT THAT BEAUTIFUL SHINY, PEACHY BLUSH.
PRESS IT GENTLY IT'S PERFECT, HEY? IT'S GOING TO BE THE PERFECT, SWEET RIPENESS.

NOW, SMELL IT. SHUT YOUR EYES.
YOU CAN ALMOST TASTE IT, HEY. LET YOUR MOUTH WATER A LITTLE, GET READY FOR THAT SUGARY TANG.

NOW YOU CAN BI—
OW!!
WHAT?!

OH MY GOD, I THINK I'VE—
—MY FUCKING TOOTH IS CHIPPED. JESUS, OW.

I WAS EMBARRASSED, SO I GOT ANGRY AT HER.
IT'S GOT A FUCKING GIANT PITT IN IT ??!!
IT'S NOT SOFT ALL THE WAY THROUGH, BABE.

YOU GOTTA TAKE IT SLOW.
WELL FUCK, BRON, I'VE NEVER EATEN ONE BEFORE HAVE I? WHY DIDN'T YOU TELL ME?

SHE LOOKED AT ME COMPLETELY BLANK THEN, AS IF I WAS A STRANGER.
I FORGOT...
I DIDN'T THINK YOU WOULDN'T KNOW.

FUCKING HELL.

HEY RACHEL?
HM?
DO YOU SWEAR AROUND MY CHILD? SHE'S STARTED DOING IT ALL THE TIME.
NOPE.

THIS IS NICE, BY THE WAY.

BEING HERE, WITH YOU AND NESS.
IT'S NICE... SEEING HOW YOU TWO ARE TOGETHER.

...I'D BEEN AVOIDING IT, ACTUALLY. FOR AGES NOW. WORK MADE THAT EASY, BUT... WELL.
WELL, YOU DID MAKE IT PRETTY OBVIOUS HOW MUCH YOU HATED BRON—

I NEVER HATED HER. AND IT WASN'T EVEN ABOUT THAT.
...I THINK I DIDN'T WANT TO SEE HOW MUCH I WAS MISSING OUT ON.
WHAT DO YOU MEAN?

I DON'T KNOW... NESSIE ALWAYS SEEMS TO HAVE SO MUCH FUN WHEN SHE'S SPENDING TIME WITH YOU.
I THOUGHT THAT IF I WAS THERE — I JUST WASN'T SURE IF IT WAS GOING TO BE LIKE A PARTY I COULDN'T JOIN IN.

... HUH.
HOW DO YOU AND BRON DO IT? HOW DO YOU GET HER TO BE SO... HAPPY?

WELL... FOR ONE THING, BRON IS MUCH, MUCH BETTER AT IT. SHE JUST KNOWS HOW TO GET ALL, LIKE, LOOSE. IN THAT WAY.
I DON'T KNOW WHAT THAT MEANS. I DON'T KNOW HOW TO MAKE THAT.
YOU DON'T HAVE TO.

IT'S NOT NECESSARILY LIKE NESSIE'S SEEING THIS MAGICAL WORLD THAT'S COMPLETELY DIFFERENT TO ADULTS.
SHE JUST... LOVES PLAY.
I GUESS YOU HAVE TO BE DOWN TO REALLY GO THERE WITH HER. AND SOMETIMES THAT'S SOMEWHERE SORT OF FERAL AND SCREAMY, AND THAT'S GREAT.

HEH–
WHAT?
I'M IMAGINING YOU KIND OF FERAL. IT'S JUST FUNNY.

SCREW YOU.

I JUST WORRY ABOUT EVERYTHING NESSIE'S BEEN EXPOSED TO.
LIKE SHE'S HAD TO BE THIS SINGULAR LITTLE SPONGE FOR ALL MY STRESS. AND EVERY-THING WITH DAVE...

ALL THE MORE REASON TO LET HER SCREAM AND RUN AROUND, MAYBE.
HM.
SOMETIMES I NOTICE HER TELLING ME EVERYTHING'S GOING TO BE FINE OR SOMETHING, AND I THINK, "GOD, I'M DOING THIS SO WRONG."

SHE'S SO... WATCHFUL.
I THINK SHE'S GOT AN OLD SOUL.
YEAH. MAYBE.

MAYBE WE JUST UNDERESTIMATE KIDS ALL OF THE TIME, THOUGH.
AND SO WE'RE SHOCKED WHEN THEY EXPRESS AN AWARENESS OR SENSI-TIVITY TO WHAT'S GOING ON.

HEY RAY?
YEAH?
YOU ARE FULL OF SHIT.

HAHA-
AND HERE YOU ARE POINTING THE FINGER AT ME FOR SAYING BAD WORDS AROUND YOUR CHILD.

MUU-UMM, WATCH MEE!
GO ON. I'M GONNA STAY HERE.

BRON, WAIT!

HEY—
YOU WALK SO FAST

BRON...

DAMMIT, WHAT'S WRONG?
NOTHING.
IT'S OK .

IT'S OBVIOUSLY NOT. WHY D'YOU LEAVE SO QUICKLY??
I THOUGHT THAT WAS FINE. I THOUGHT IT'S BEEN FINE. TELL ME WHAT'S UP.

...THESE PAST FEW WEEKS AT GROUP—
IT HASN'T BEEN FINE, GRACE.
WHAT DO YOU MEAN?

I HATE TALKING ABOUT THIS SHIT.
. . .

OK, FINE. SIT HERE FOR A SEC.
SO... YOU KNOW THOSE TIMES WHEN MUM'S MAD AT ONE OF US?

AND SHE'S BEHAVING LIKE EVERYTHING'S FINE —
— WHEN ACTUALLY SHE CAN BARELY LOOK AT YOU.
HA, OH GOD, YEAH.

AND INSTEAD OF CALLING IT, EVERYONE ELSE IS ALSO ACTING LIKE IT'S ALL FINE —
OR WORSE, THEY'RE CONVINCED THAT EVERYTHING ACTUALLY IS FINE.

AND SO YOU END UP FEELING CRAZY.
. . .

WELL, IT CAN BE LIKE THAT FOR ME A LOT, EXCEPT IT'S LIKE... EVERYONE'S MUM.
AND THEY'RE MAD AT ME FOR JUST EXISTING.

BUT... I DON'T GET IT.
WHEN I TOLD EVERYONE LAST MONTH YOU WERE JOINING US, THEY WERE ALL REALLY INTO IT.

LIKE, EVERYONE WAS ACTUALLY REALLY KEEN TO MEET YOU.
MIRANDA HANGS AROUND SPECIFICALLY TO SAY HEY.

MIRANDA'S STARING EVERY TIME I'M AROUND. I THOUGHT IT WOULD GET BETTER AFTER THE FIRST WEEK, BUT SHE'S ALWAYS UP-AND-DOWNING ME AS IF I CAN'T SEE HER DOING IT.
I DON'T KNOW, GRACE—

THIS SHIT, IT USED TO MAKE ME FEEL LIKE I WAS GOING INSANE.
AND WHEN I MET RAY, IT WAS LIKE SHE JUST WALKED IN AND RIPPED BACK THE CURTAIN AND WAS LIKE, "YEAH, I CAN TOTALLY SEE WHAT'S GOING ON, AND I CAN TOTALLY SEE WHAT IT'S DOING TO YOU."

IT MADE ME FEEL LIKE I COULD BREATHE AGAIN.

SO, GO BACK TO HER
THAT'S NOT WHAT I'M SAY-ING. I'M SORRY, I DIDN'T MEAN TO MAKE IT SEEM LIKE—

I THINK WHAT I'M TRYING TO SAY IS — THOSE TIMES, WHEN PEOPLE ARE ACTING LIKE I'M THIS BIG FUCKING ODDITY —
I WANT TO FEEL LIKE YOU'RE THERE WITH ME. NOT ON THE OTHER SIDE OF THE GLASS.

DO YOU THINK YOU CAN DO THAT?

...YEAH. OK
I'LL TRY.

LET'S GO HOME?

GRACIE, HOW WAS GROUP TODAY?
GRACE, PHONE.

OK, OK.
SO, GROUP?

RIGHT, YEAH—
IT WAS FINE..?

IT WAS HARD, ACTUALLY. IT WAS HARD WITH EVERYONE.

THE YOUTH GROUP IS A GOOD BUNCH OF KIDS.
THEY MAKE ME FEEL LIKE AN OUTSIDER.
I'M SURE IF YOU GIVE IT SOME MORE TIME —

IT'S ALREADY BEEN A MONTH.
I DON'T WANT TO GO BACK.

WELL THEY WOULD VIEW YOU AS AN OUTSIDER, IF YOU HAVEN'T BEEN PART OF THEIR PATH UNTIL NOW.
IF IT WAS ANYONE ELSE, MUM —

IT IS POSSIBLE THAT YOU ARE DETERMINED TO STAY ON THE OUTSIDE.
IN WHICH CASE, BLAMING OTHERS ISN'T FAIR OR APPROPRIATE.

...
GRACIE, HOW IS MIRANDA? DID SHE APPLY FOR THAT EXCHANGE PROGRAM I SENT TO HER MUM?

I... UH, I THINK SHE MIGHT HAVE?
SERIOUSLY??THAT'S IT?

THE WAY I'M TREATED IS ALL MY FAULT, END OF CONVERSATION, AND THEN WE'RE MOVING ONTO NICER THINGS?

GRACIE? REMEMBER THE CONVERSATION WE LITERALLY JUST HAD??

. . .
NO...?

FINE. FUCK.
I'M GOING TO BED.

KNOCK
KNOCK

BRON...?

...

RAY..?
CAN I ASK ABOUT BRON?
... OK...

IS SHE - I MEAN, HAS SHE CONTACTED YOU? HAVE YOU HEARD ANYTHING?
NO. I LEFT HER VOICEMAILS AT FIRST, AND TEXTS. BUT I STARTED TO FEEL LIKE I WAS HARASSING HER, SO I STOPPED.
HMM.

... IT'S JUST - I WAS THINKING -
YOU SAID HER FAMILY WERE...
WHAT'S IT LIKE FOR SOMEONE LIKE... YOU KNOW...
WHAT'S IT LIKE FOR SOMEONE LIKE BRON, IN THAT KIND OF FIRE AND BRIMSTONE SHIT?

LAST TIME, THEY TRIED TO GET HER TO TALK TO SOME PSYCH-DUDE CONNECTED TO THEIR CHURCH COMMUNITY.
I THINK EVERYONE JUST WORKED REAL HARD TO CONVINCE HER SHE WASN'T REALLY TRANS, AND SHE JUST NEEDED TO BEG CHRIST FOR FORGIVENESS OR WHATEVER THE HELL.

LIKE, I KNOW SHE'S NOT THE PIC-TURE OF PERFECT MENTAL HEALTH.
BUT IF EVERYONE IN YOUR ENVIRONMENT IS TRYING TO TELL YOU THAT THE THING YOU ARE DOESN'T ACTUALLY EXIST... THAT'S NOT GOOD FOR A PERSON.

...CAN I SAY SOMETHING STUPID?
YOU USUALLY CAN.
JUST... ALL THIS TIME. I GUESS I THOUGHT BRON WAS JUST BEING OVERLY SENSITIVE.

THAT IS STUPID.
I KNOW. I'M SORRY.
IT'S NOT ME YOU NEEDA APOLOGIZE TO.

ALL THIS STUFF, IT FEELS LIKE IT TAKES ME FOREVER TO GET, BUT IT DOESN'T SEEM TO BE DIFFICULT FOR NESS AT ALL, YOU KNOW? SHE JUST TAKES IT IN HER STRIDE.
I KNOW, I WATCH HER DOING THAT, TOO. YOU KNOW WHAT SHE SAID TO ME THE OTHER DAY? SHE SAID I'M STILL FUN, EVEN WHEN I'M SLUMPY.

AND ARE YOU?
AM I WHAT? SLUMPY OR FUN?
EITHER, I GUESS.
I AM THE SADDEST SLUMP THAT EVER SLUMPED. NO FUN.

OH, WHATEVER. NESSIE ALWAYS HAS A GOOD TIME WITH YOU. I'M SURE YOU'RE PULLING SOME KIND OF AMAZING ADVENTURE FROM SOMEWHERE.
I DUNNO. I TOLD YOU, IT WAS MOSTLY BRON WHO COULD GET THAT MAGIC SHIT GOING. I'M PROBABLY AS BORING AS YOU, WITHOUT HER NOW.
OH THANKS VERY MUCH.

...DO YOU THINK BRON'S OK, THEN?

I HONESTLY HAVE NO IDEA. I DON'T KNOW WHY SHE WOULD EVER GO BACK TO THOSE PEOPLE.
MAYBE SHE STILL LOVES THEM? MAYBE IT WAS HARD FOR HER TO JUST RENOUNCE HER RELIGION, I DON'T KNOW.

SERIOUSLY? YOU'RE PUTTING STOCK IN THE WHOLE GOD THING?
WELL, WHY NOT? I'M JUST GUESSING.
DO YOU GET IT, ALL THAT RELIGIOUS STUFF?

OF COURSE NOT. SUNDAYS ARE GROCERIES AND LAUNDRY AND JAMIE OLIVER AT SEVEN, YOU KNOW THAT.
BEING RAISED TO PRAY AND REPENT AND BE IN COMMUNITY LIKE THAT — I DON'T KNOW THAT LIFE... MAYBE THOSE TIES ARE HARD TO CUT.

SHE SAID SHE NEVER WANTED TO SEE HER FAMILY AGAIN.
SHE SAID THAT ME AND NESSIE WOULD ALWAYS BE ENOUGH FAMILY FOR HER
YES, WELL, PEOPLE SAY A LOT OF SHIT. LET'S GO INSIDE? IT'S TOO COLD NOW.

YOU REALLY HATE THE RELIGIOUS PIECE, HEY.

MAYBE.
I THINK I'M MORE TERRIFIED OF IT, ACTUALLY.

REALLY? YOU HAVEN'T ALWAYS BEEN.
I THINK IT'S BEEN SINCE I'VE KNOWN BRON.
WHAT DO YOU MEAN?

I DUNNO ANYMORE IF IT'S THE GOD STUFF THAT SCARES ME —
OR IF IT'S JUST THAT THERE'S THIS HUGE PART OF BRON I TOTALLY CAN'T ACCESS.
LIKE I'VE PUT ALL MY SENSE OF BELONGING INTO THIS PERSON THAT I ACTUALLY DON'T UNDER-STAND AT ALL.

I THINK IT'S FOOLISH TO PUT ALL YOUR BELONGING INTO ANY ONE PERSON.
YOU DID. WITH DAVE.
EXACTLY.

NESSIE... ASKS ABOUT BRON A LOT.
I USED TO FEEL CONCERNED ABOUT HER BEING IN BRON'S CARE. I FELT LIKE I DIDN'T SIGN UP FOR THAT WHEN YOU SAID YOU'D TAKE NESS TWICE A WEEK.

YEAH, YOU MADE YOUR CONCERNS PRETTY CLEAR
BUT, I DON'T KNOW. THINGS HAVE BEEN...
DIFFERENT. SINCE SHE LEFT.

...WHY DON'T YOU GO OVER AND CHECK IN ON HER?
SHE DOESN'T WANT ME TO. SHE DOESN'T WANT ME ANYMORE.
DID SHE SAY THAT?

YEAH...
I DON'T KNOW, ACTUALLY.
YOU SHOULD TALK TO HER. IT'S MESSED UP THAT YOU STILL DON'T KNOW. YOU NEED TO KNOW.

I'M SCARED. IF SHE'S ACTUALLY SURE SHE DOESN'T WANT TO BE TOGETHER—
...I DON'T WANT TO HEAR THAT

YOU NEED TO KNOW.

ANYWAY. NESSIE ASKS ABOUT BRON A LOT.

TEN YEARS...
I WAITED TEN YEARS

NO MORE WAITING –

WE HAVE THE REST OF OUR LIVES –

WE'LL NEVER WAIT AGAIN

OH GOD, THIS IS TOO MUCH –
OI! SHHH!!

YOU LOVED THAT.
I DIDN'T LOVE IT.

THE BIT WHERE HE FINALLY COMES HOME AFTER THE WAR?
YOU WERE ALL GOO-GOO EYES.
WELL, OK, IT WAS NICE I LIKE THAT ROMO-SHIT SOMETIMES, SO WHAT. ME AND EVERY OTHER GIRL IN THE PLACE.

IT'S ONLY ROMANTIC BECAUSE IT ENDS AT THE RIGHT MOMENT, BEFORE THEY GET ALL WORN DOWN BY THEIR ACTUAL SHIT—
OK, MAYBE NOT EVERYTHING IS ABOUT YOU AND YOUR EMO BREAKUP?

I WASN'T TALKING ABOUT—
WHATEVER.
YOU WANT ICECREAM? LET'S GET ICECREAM, MY TREAT.

I LITERALLY ALWAYS WANT ICECREAM. BUT THE MOVIE WAS YOUR TREAT. I DO HAVE SOME MONEY.
COME ON, JUST LET ME. WHAT FLAVOR?

UH... FINE. OREO, WAFFLE CONE.
GREAT.
HI - CAN I GET ONE OREO, ONE PISTACHIO. WAFFLE CONES.

WHAT'S UP WITH YOU?

YOU KNOW, YOU'RE BEING REAL EXTRA NICE. AND IT'S WIGGING ME OUT.
I DUNNO WHAT YOU MEAN.

YOU'VE JUST BEEN ALL... AGREEING WITH WHATEVER I WANNA DO. ALL DAY.
FEELS LIKE YOU'RE... LIKE, BUTTERING ME UP TO TELL ME SOMETHING BAD.
YEAH... WELL... WHY DON'T WE SIT. HERE.

IT'S... YOU'RE MOVING OUT, AREN'T YOU.
...

JEEZ BRON!! YOU'VE TAKEN ME ON A CUTE MALL TRIP SO I DON'T FREAK OUT AT YOU, BECAUSE YOU'RE LEAVING. AGAIN.
GRACIE, PLEASE –
THIS IS SO FUCKING PATRONIZING!

IT'S NOT POSSIBLE THAT I ALSO JUST WANTED TO SPEND SOME TIME WITH YOU?
I'M NOT A FUCKING CHILD, YOU KNOW.
WELL, MAYBE YOU'RE ACTING LIKE ONE RIGHT NOW.

OH, FUCK YOU. GO HAVE A NICE MAKE-UP WITH YOUR COOL ASIAN GIRLFRIEND.
THAT'S NOT WHAT'S HAPPENING.

I'VE FOUND AN APARTMENT IN THE WEST. I'M GOING TO TRY LIVING ON MY OWN, SAVING SOME MONEY.
AND I GOT A WINTER JOB. AT A FLORIST.

COOL, WHY ARE YOU TELLING ME THIS?
BECAUSE I DON'T WANT YOU TO THINK I'M JUST PISSING OFF.
THAT'S WHAT YOU DID LAST TIME. THAT'S LITERALLY WHAT YOU ARE DOING RIGHT NOW.

I—
THIS IS TOTALLY DIFFERENT. I'M GOING TO CALL YOU—
I'M GOING TO SEND YOU EMAILS, AND I'LL SET UP A SPOT WHERE YOU COULD COME CRASH SOMETIMES.

HOW ABOUT THIS.
YOU MOVE OUT, AND FIGURE OUT HOW TO GET YOUR ACTUAL SHIT TOGETHER.
THEN YOU CAN TELL ME WHAT YOU'RE GOING TO DO.

I'M TAKING THE BUS HOME.

OH IF I WAS A SNAIL

I'D MAR-RY A CRAB—

'CUZ A SNAIL'S GOT NO ARMS

AND A CRAB CAN GRAB

OH IF I WAS A SNAIL
I'D MARRY A CRAB

CUZ A SNAIL'S GOT NO ARMS
AND A CRAB CAN GRAB

NO I DON'T WANNA BEEE–

THAT SNAIL NO MOOORE

THAT WAS A REALLY GOOD ONE, BUB!
MUMMA HELPED ME A LOT WITH THE RHYMING. I CHOSE THE CRAB PART.

HUH, FANCY THAT.
GOOD FOR HER.

COMING DOWN!!
FLOP
HAAAHAHAAAA!!

AGAIN!
I NEED A REST MY DARLING, MY ARMS ARE TIRED.

... AUNTIE RAY?
YEAH?
WHEN WILL YOU STOP BEING SAD?

I DON'T KNOW. IT FEELS LIKE IT WILL BE FOREVER —
BUT I GUARANTEE IT'LL BE LESS TIME THAN FOREVER.

MUMMA SAID WHEN SHE WAS REALLY SAD, SHE PRETENDED LIKE SHE WAS A DIFFERENT PERSON THAT WASN'T SO SAD.
SHE TOLD YOU THAT?
YEP. I DON'T REMEMBER SO MUCH. BUT SHE SAID SHE CALLED HERSELF MISS. G LIKE THE MISS. G ON T.V — THE LADY WHO'S ALWAYS DANCING.

THAT WORKOUT COMMERCIAL LADY ON CHANNEL TEN? OH MY GOD, I REMEMBER HER – HA!
"NOBODY GONNA MESS WITH ME, I'M A DO-ER, I'M MISS G–"
WOW, I AM DEFINITELY GOING TO TALK TO HER ABOUT THIS.

MAYBE IF YOU JUST DO SOMEBODY DIFF-ERENT FOR A BIT, YOU'D FEEL LESS SAD.
... SURE, WHY NOT. WHO WOULD I BE, THEN?

I DON'T KNOW...
SOMEONE WHO'S ALWAYS DOING JUST FINE.
WHAT ABOUT IF YOU WERE ANGELA. WITH RED HAIR.

ANGELA FROM PLAYSCHOOL? NAH, I DON'T WANNA BE SOME PEPPY WHITE LADY.
WELL WHAT ABOUT HENNY PENNY.
THE HEN??
SHE'S BRAVE! AND SHE HAS NICE FEATHERS.

IT'S TRUE, SHE'S BRAVE. ALL RIGHT, THAT'S WHAT'S UP TODAY THEN. PLEASED TO MEET YOU, NESSIE.
PLEASED TO MEET YOU, AUNTIE HENNY PENNY!

WHAT NOW, SWEETPEA?
WE GO TO THE PARK??

IT'S RAINNING!
YOU DON'T JUST WANNA WATCH A MOVIE OR SOMETHING??

IT'S NOT SO RAINY!!
HENNY PENNY IS A BRAVE AND ADVENTUROUS HEN!!

SECOND ON THE LEFT. CALL ME IF THE HEAT'S NOT WORKING.
OK, THANK YOU.

HI - YEAH, THE HEAT'S NOT ON.

OK...

OK–

OK.

SEEE??

NOT SO RAINY!!

OH IF I WAS A CRAB-
OOPS, I MEAN-

OH IF I WAS A SNAIL~

KNOCK
KNOCK

...

N'T WANNA BEEEEEE—

THAT SNAIL NO MOOOOREE

OK!!
I'M CLIMBING UP TO MY ROOST NOW!

YOU GOTTA COME AND GET ME OR I'LL JUST FLY AWAY!!

NESSIE?

AUNTIE BRON!!!

O O O O O O A A

FOR THE FIRST COUPLE OF YEARS, THE DIFFERENCES BETWEEN ME AND BRON MADE US FUCKING VORACIOUS.

AS IF THEY MADE UP THIS GREAT SPRAWLING LANDSCAPE THAT WE COULD FLOOD ACROSS, TOWARDS EACH OTHER.

SO MUCH GROUND TO COVER.

IT KEPT US UP AT NIGHT - TRYING TO REVEAL AND EXAMINE ALL THE PIECES THAT SEEMED TOTALLY ALIEN, TOTALLY FASCINATING.

LATER ON, THAT BIG SPACE BECAME ALL MIXED UP WITH LETHARGY, AND SOMETHING LIKE HOPELESSNESS.

LIKE THERE WAS NO AMOUNT OF STORYTELLING OR SHARING OR TALKING THAT WOULD CLOSE THE GAP.

I... UH—
I GOT AN APARTMENT. ON THE WEST SIDE.

THAT'S GREAT, GOOD FOR YOU.
THANKS...

SNAP

SHE READ A WHOLE BOOK ON HER OWN THE OTHER DAY.
NO SHIT. WHICH ONE?
THE MR. POTATO ONE WITH THE FOLD-OUT BITS.

OF COURSE, A MASTERPIECE. DAMN, I FEEL LIKE SHE'S GROWN SO MUCH IN THREE MONTHS.
YEAH, WELL, THEY GROW FAST. YOU BLINK AND YOU MISS A LOT.

...

HAHA
WHAT??
SORRY—

WHAT'S FUNNY?
SORRY - NOTHING'S FUNNY. REALLY. IT'S JUST - I THINK I'M NERVOUS OR SOMETHING.
I DUNNO WHAT TO SAY TO YOU.

LIKE, THE LAST TIME I SAW YOU I WAS LITERALLY CRYING IN MY UNDERWEAR ON THE STREET.
I MEAN, FUCK.

YOU SHOULD'VE CALLED TO TELL ME YOU WERE COMING.
I KNOW. I KEPT MEANING TO, AND THEN PSYCHING MYSELF OUT -
YOU SHOULD'VE CALLED. IN GENERAL.

I KNOW.

...YOU KNOW, ALL WINTER I'VE PICTURED YOU COMING HOME, OR LIKE, COMING HERE.
I DON'T - I GUESS THIS ISN'T HOME FOR YOU ANYMORE, BUT ANYWAY -
EVERYTIME I PICTURED IT, IT WOULD INVOLVE ALL THIS HUGGING AND CRYING -

NOT LIKE, WITH ME UP A FUCKING TREE. OR ON THE BEAMONT TRACKS.
BUT HERE WE ARE. I DON'T KNOW WHAT I'M DOING HERE.

I JUST... DON'T KNOW WHAT TO SAY.
CAN YOU... DO YOU HAVE ANYTHING TO SAY?

... I REALLY MISSED YOU.
YEAH.
I MISSED YOU, TOO.

SWING

THIS ISN'T US GETTING BACK TOGETHER, IS IT.

RIGHT? THIS ISN'T HOW IT GOES.
... NO.
I MEAN YES. IT'S NOT.

... DID YOU COME HERE TO TELL ME THAT?
I DON'T KNOW.
I CAME BECAUSE I WANTED TO SAY HI TO YOU AND NESSIE. AND TO SAY SORRY.

FOR DISAPPEARING.
FOR EVERYTHING.

SIGH-
WHAT ARE YOU FEELING. RIGHT NOW?
CURRENTLY NOTHING. LATER, PROBABLY PLENTY.

SOMETIMES I WISH WE COULD JUST GO BACK TO THE TIME WHEN AMANDA WAS STILL A JERK, AND YOU STILL LOVED ME, AND EVERYTHING WAS STILL KIND OF NORMAL.

WELL, I STILL LOVE YOU.
I DON'T KNOW WHAT TO DO WITH THAT, BRON.

YOU'RE RIGHT, I'M SORRY.
... BUT AMANDA'S STILL A JERK, RIGHT?
NOT SO MUCH, IT TURNS OUT. THINGS ARE REALLY CHANGING EVERYWHERE.

HUH. DOES SHE STILL HATE ME?
NOT AS MUCH AS YOU'D THINK.

BUT IF YOU'VE ACTUALLY BROKEN MY HEART – AND I THINK YOU MIGHT'VE – THEN IT'S BASICALLY HER JOB TO HATE YOU A BIT. AT LEAST FOR A WHILE.
SLIDE
... THAT'S FAIR ENOUGH.

AM I STILL... I MEAN, HOW WOULD YOU FEEL ABOUT –
WHAT?
DO I STILL GET TO BE AUNTIE BRON SOMETIMES?

...
THIS IS THE PART WHERE I WANT TO SAY, YES, OF COURSE. BUT, I THINK IT'S MY TURN TO TAKE SOME TIME NOW.

BUT NESSIE'S NOT GOING TO FORGET YOU ANYTIME SOON. THERE'S TIME. AND YOU'RE YOU. SHE'S OBSESSED WITH YOU.
I'M OBSESSED WITH HER.
I KNOW.

I JUST... NEED SOME TIME TO GET MY SHIT ACTUALLY BACK TOGETHER.
TELL ME ABOUT IT.

I PROBABLY NEED TO LIKE, SPEND SOME TIME BEING ANGRY AT YOU—
AND PAY AN ENTIRE WINTER'S WORTH OF HEATING—
AND HANG OUT WITH SOME ACTUAL FRIENDS. WHO AREN'T MY SISTER.

YUP, ME TOO WITH THE FRIENDS.
SO YOU SAW GRACIE? HOW WAS IT?
YEAH, SHE'S... WELL, SHE'S SIXTEEN NOW.
SHE'S REALLY SMART, AND HAS A BUNCH OF FRIENDS... AND SHE'S UPSET THAT I LEFT. YELLED AT ME, WHEN I TOLD HER.

HA, SHE AND I COULD MAKE A CLUB.
GIVE HER TIME, BRON. SHE'LL COME AROUND. SHE MUST LOVE YOU A LOT, IF SHE'S REAL MAD YOU LEFT.

THANKS.
YEAH.

DAMMIT!!
RRINNGG!

AMANDA, HEY.
YEAH, EVERYTHING'S FINE.

YEAH, WE'RE AT THE MALL RIGHT NOW. HM? YEAH, SHE HAD SOME CHEESE AND BISCUITS BEFORE WE LEFT.
UH YEAH, FINE – HALF AN HOUR? OK.
OK, BYE.

...

...DO WE SAY GOODBYE BEFORE OR AFTER DROPPING NESSIE HOME?
MAYBE... AFTER? IF YOU—I MEAN, ONLY IF, YOU KNOW—
YEAH, NO IT'S FINE. AFTER WORKS.
AFTER IS GOOD.

NESSIE—
TIME TO GO, SWEETHEART.

## ACKNOWLEDGEMENTS

Thank you to Wai-yant Li, Tommi Parrish, my parents Janet & Charles, and my sister Cesca — for much more than I can say on a page.

Thank you to Eli Tareq El Bechelany-Lynch, for their care and their indispensable edits.

Thank you to these people (in no particular order), who supported me with their company, food, opinions, encouragement, and advice during the making of this comic:

The Li family (Wai-Yant, Eva, William, Ci, Wilson & Leah Q)
Yarijey Techer
Faraz Abdullah
Sorraya Guembhyt
Tariq Ali Jamal
Shae Beeman
Yousra Andre
Griffin Ferril
Alex Felicitas
Toino Dumas
Camerin Cobb
Betty Buckrich
Toby Lukin
Eve Melgaard
Annie Koyama
Maya Penn
Marc Pearson
Samia Marshy
Tracy Hurren
Jillian Tamaki
Dr. A Rubineau
The Montreal Sacred Harp choir
Prof. Ken Briscoe,
and the scriptwriting class of '19
Alessandra Sternfeld
Gary Groth, Jacq Cohen,
and the Fantagraphics team

EDITOR: Gary Groth
EDITORIAL ASSISTANCE: Conrad Groth
PRODUCTION: Paul Baresh and Covey
ASSOCIATE PUBLISHER: Eric Reynolds
PUBLISHER: Gary Groth



ISBN: 978-1-68396-426-1
Library of Congress Control Number: 2020948305
First Fantagraphics Books edition: May 2021
Printed in China

FANTAGRAPHICS BOOKS, INC.
7563 Lake City Way NE
Seattle, WA 98115
www.fantagraphics.com
facebook.com/fantagraphics
@fantagraphics.com